Messiah

The 70-Week Prophecy and the Gospel of Luke

James Rafferty

To order additional copies call 1-877-585-1111 or visit www.lightbearers.org

Contents

Daniel and the Gospel of Luke

The book of Luke is an inspired, systematic, deliberately historic verification of the Messiahship of Jesus Christ. It is written for the purpose of persuading all who are "excellent" (strong and noble) that Jesus Christ is Messiah (Luke 1:3).

The first three chapters of Luke identify the time of Christ's birth and baptism. This historical account makes an intentional connection between this world-altering event and a prophecy tucked away in the prophetic book of Daniel. I am referring specifically to Daniel 8 and 9, where we find the 2300-day/70-week prophecy.

Even the biblically savvy have missed what could be called a "back door" connection between these two portions of Scripture. There are at least seven significant links between Luke and Daniel:

1. Luke, like Daniel, focuses on historical facts and events surrounding the Messiah.

2. Both Daniel and Luke have prophetic ties.

3. Surprisingly, Luke and Daniel are the only books of the Bible that identify the angel Gabriel by name.

4. These are the only books of the Bible that identify two Roman Caesars (Luke mentions Augustus and Tiberius by name).

5. Both books introduce Caesar Augustus as a "raiser of taxes" (Daniel 11:20; Luke 3:1).

6. Both books describe the anointing of the Messiah.

7. Both books describe the death of the Messiah.

These historic, prophetic, and Messianic details connect Daniel to Luke in a unique way. It is evident that Luke was telling his version of the Jesus story with an eye on Daniel's prophecy. The fact that God inspired these two Bible writers to record the name of Gabriel is no insignificant detail. The "Gabriel connection" alone strongly suggests a link between these two books that is singular and meaningful.

The Gabriel Connection

Daniel, Luke, and Gabriel—great names for three boys if you're looking to build a family—but greater still if you're looking to build an understanding of Bible truth. By having Gabriel intentionally identify himself in the book of Luke, God elicits a query, "Where have we heard of this angel before?" And the question leads to only one place in Scripture: to Daniel 8 and 9 (Daniel 8:16; 9:21; Luke 1:19, 26). The "Gabriel connection" is no coincidence, because in both books Gabriel's appearance is directly connected to the entrance of the Messiah into the world.

In Daniel, Gabriel is connected to the 2300-day/70-week prophecy that is *predictive* of the Messiah. In Luke, Gabriel is connected to the same 70-week portion of the 2300-day prophecy that is *fulfilled* by the Messiah. The Messiah is the central focus of Daniel's four major historical prophetic visions. The

Messiah is:

1. The "Stone" of Daniel 2.

2. The "Son of man" in Daniel 7.

3. The "Prince of princes" in Daniel 8.

4. The " Prince of the covenant" in Daniel 11.

The Messiah is central to Luke's gospel, as well. He verifies the following:

1. The birth of the Messiah.

2. The anointing and ministry of the Messiah.

3. The death of the Messiah.

4. The resurrection of the Messiah.

The Gabriel connection is simple, yet evidential of a significant relation between two books written hundreds of years apart. In Daniel, Gabriel comes to foretell. In Luke, he comes to announce, confirming that what he had foretold to Daniel is about to happen.

Troubling Prophecies

Both in Luke and Daniel, Gabriel is the one sent from heaven to communicate to Planet Earth vital information regarding the Messiah.

In Luke, Gabriel explains the relationship between John the Baptist and the Messiah. He informs an incredulous Zacharias that he and his wife Elizabeth will give birth to the forerunner of the Messiah, John the Baptist. A short time later, Gabriel is again sent by God to a virgin named Mary to inform her that she will conceive and bring forth the Son of the Highest, the Messiah Himself, without intimately knowing a man (Luke 1:11-20; 26-38).

In Daniel, Gabriel explains the relationship between a seemingly mysterious time prophecy, 2300 days in duration and a subdivision of that 2300 days, 70 weeks in length. In them he outlines, point by point, when the Messiah will come, be anointed, be cut-off, and confirm the covenant (Daniel 9:24-27).

In Luke, Gabriel's message troubles Zacharias so much that he expresses doubt regarding its feasibility, specifically the part where he and his aging, barren wife are to give birth to a son. His doubt leads to a heavenly "time-out"—nine-months of silence for his failure to believe the words of Gabriel.

Gabriel's message causes Daniel trouble as well. At first he cannot make sense of the 2300 days and how it relates to a prophecy in the book of Jeremiah designating a 70-year time cap for the termination of Babylonian captivity. Distraught, Daniel literally becomes sick over the whole thing. Here is his account of the experience:

"And I Daniel fainted, and was sick certain days; afterward I rose up, and did the king's business; and I was astonished at the vision, but none understood it" (Daniel 8:27).

A short time later Daniel sought God in prayer for understanding—always a good thing when studying prophetic messages of the Bible. By this time Daniel had compared the 2300-day prophecy in Daniel 8 to the 70-year prophecy of Babylonian captivity given in Jeremiah 25:12. Now Daniel needed talk-time with God to understand what it all meant:

"In the first year of Darius the son of Ahasuerus, of the seed of the Medes, which was made king over the realm of the Chaldeans; In the first year of his reign I Daniel understood by books the number of the years, whereof the word of the Lord came to Jeremiah the prophet, that he would accomplish seventy years in the desolations of Jerusalem. And I set my face unto the Lord God, to seek by prayer and supplications, with fasting, and sackcloth, and ashes" (Daniel 9:1-3).

Bathed in humility, Daniel's prayer is the fulcrum for understanding any and all prophecy. Daniel prays with:

1. Humility of knowledge (Daniel 9:2).
2. Humility of actions (Daniel 9:3).
3. Humility of attitude (Daniel 9:5-18).
4. Humility of motive (Daniel 9:19).

Daniel 9 is a revelation to us of the power of prayer! And what else could we expect from this humble, powerful prayer but an equally powerful answer. Gabriel is commissioned to deliver the answer. He does this by bringing to Daniel a revelation of the humility of the Messiah.

Clarification

The answer to Daniel's humble prayer comes personally, visibly, and "swiftly" in the form of Gabriel, the highest-ranking angel in heaven. Here is Daniel's first-hand account of his Gabriel connection:

"Now while I was speaking, praying, and confessing my sin and the sin of my people Israel, and presenting my supplication before the LORD my God for the holy mountain of my God, yes, while I was speaking in prayer, the man Gabriel, whom I had seen in the vision at the beginning, being caused to fly swiftly, reached me about the time of the evening offering. And he informed me, and talked with me, and said, 'O Daniel, I have now come forth to give you skill to understand. At the beginning of your supplications the command went out, and I have come to tell you, for you are greatly beloved; therefore consider the matter, and understand the vision: Seventy weeks are determined for your people and for your holy city, to finish the transgression, to make an end of sins, to make reconciliation for iniquity, to bring in everlasting righteousness, to seal up vision and prophecy, and to anoint the Most Holy. Know therefore and understand, that from the going forth of the command to restore and build Jerusalem until Messiah the Prince, there shall be seven weeks and sixty-two weeks; the street shall be built again, and the wall, even in troublesome times. And after the sixty-two weeks Messiah shall be cut off, but not for Himself; and the people of the prince who is to come shall destroy the city and the sanctuary. The end of it shall be with a flood, and till the end of the war desolations are determined. Then He shall confirm a covenant with many for one week; but in the middle of the week He shall bring an end to sacrifice and offering. And on the wing of abominations shall be one who makes desolate, even until the consummation, which is determined, is poured out on the desolate'" (Daniel 9:20-27, NKJV).

These eight verses highlight the central message of Daniel's book and, in essence, the entire Bible. They speak, in prophetic language, of the coming of the Messiah, the Savior of the world. One thought shines out crystal clear: "after threescore and two weeks shall Messiah be cut off, but not for Himself."

"Messiah" (Hebrew) refers to "Christ" (Greek),

which in both instances means, "Anointed One." Christ's anointing occurred publicly at His baptism by the Holy Spirit. Finally, He would be "cut off," referring to His death for the sins of the world (John 1:29). Christ died for us, "not for Himself." His death was for "the iniquity of us all" (Isaiah 53:6). His mission was to "taste death" for all, every man, woman, and child conceived on Planet Earth (Hebrews 2:9).

The four verses of Daniel 9:24-27 (NKJV) offer a prophetic picture of a series of events that relate to the Messiah and the Jerusalem temple. Each verse predicts a historical event concerning the Messiah and the temple. The outline looks like this:

Verse 24:

Messiah—"Finish the transgression, to make an end of sins, to make reconciliation for iniquity, to bring in everlasting righteousness, to seal up vision and prophecy, and to anoint the Most Holy."

Jerusalem Temple—"Seventy weeks are determined for your people and for your holy city."

Verse 25:

Messiah—"Know therefore and understand, that from the going forth of the command to restore and build Jerusalem until Messiah the Prince, there shall be seven weeks and sixty-two weeks."

Jerusalem Temple—"The street shall be built again, and the wall. Even in troublesome times."

Verse 26:

Messiah—"Messiah shall be cut off, but not for Himself."

Jerusalem Temple—"And the people of the prince who is to come shall destroy the city and the sanctuary. The end of it shall be with a flood, and till the end of the war desolations are determined."

Verse 27:

Messiah—"Then He shall confirm a covenant with many for one week; but in the middle of the week He shall bring an end to sacrifice and offering."

Jerusalem Temple—"And on the wing of abominations shall be one who makes desolate, even until the consummation, which is determined, is poured out on the desolate."

In Summary:

Messiah will take care of our sin, transgression and iniquity; bring in righteousness; seal up the vision and prophecy; anoint the Most Holy; be baptized with the Spirit after 69 prophetic weeks; be cut off/crucified in the middle of the 70th prophetic week, bringing the ceremonial animal sacrifices to an end.

The Jerusalem Temple will be rebuilt within seven prophetic weeks, even in difficult times, then be destroyed by the Romans and lay desolate until the very end of time when the desolations determined are poured out on the lost.

This Messiah-Temple outline given by Gabriel is key to a correct interpretation of the 70-week prophecy. Let's take a closer look.

The 70 Weeks

Most of us know what it's like to try to chew a chunk of food too big for our mouth. Smaller, bite-size pieces are easier to handle and it's the same with Bible prophecy. This is why Gabriel breaks the 2300-day prophecy into smaller bite-size subdivisions of time marked by various events so that this prophecy can be better assimilated.

The first portion of time marked off is 70 weeks. This portion of the 2300 days was allotted to the children of Israel to "finish the transgression, and to make an end of sins, and to make reconciliation for iniquity, and to bring in everlasting righteousness, and to seal up the vision and prophecy, and to anoint the most Holy" (Daniel 9:24). The 70 weeks are further subdivided into three basic pieces:

1. 69 weeks until the Messiah the anointed One.

2. 7 weeks for the rebuilding of Jerusalem and the Temple.

3. 1 week, the final week of the 70 weeks, during which Messiah will be cut off and the covenant will be confirmed.

Chart 1

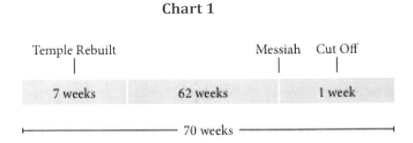

Next, let's calculate the 70 weeks in days:

70 prophetic weeks x 7 days in a week = 490 prophetic days.

Now we are ready, with the aid of the Holy Spirit, to know and understand this Messianic prophecy. The key to understanding it is the Messiah Himself. The prophecy states that from the going forth of the decree to rebuild Jerusalem "until Messiah the Prince, there shall be seven weeks and sixty-two weeks" (Daniel 9:25, NKJV). The 69 prophetic weeks (483 prophetic days) is a key time marker of the 70-week time period because it takes us to the Messiah.

If we take this prophetic time literally, Daniel could have looked for the Messiah to appear 69 weeks or 483 literal days (about 16 months) from the decree to rebuild Jerusalem. This decree was brought forth in Daniel's time, but the Messiah was not. This tells us that the prophetic time designated was not literal time. Then how is this prophetic time to be calculated?

The answer can be found in a biblical rule of prophetic interpretation simply called the "day-for-a-year principle." There are times when God gives prophecies in which He designates each day as one year. This happened when His people wandered through the wilderness for 40 years. God gave them this prophetic time period of wandering based on the 40 days that the spies were searching out the land. Each day represented one year. The Bible says:

"And your children shall wander in the wilderness forty years, and bear your whoredoms, until your carcasses be wasted in the wilderness. After the number of the days in which you searched the land, even forty days, each day for a year, shall you bear your iniquities, even forty years, and you shall know My breach of promise" (Numbers 14:33, 34).

God "appointed" this same day-for-a-year principle

in the prophetic book of Ezekiel to illustrate the judgment that He prophesied against Jerusalem (Ezekiel 4:6).

Applying the day-for-a-year principle takes the application of this prophecy to the Messiah 483 years from the decree to rebuild Jerusalem. This timeframe matches the historical account of the birth and baptism of Christ, as we will see in the book of Luke.

So based on the principle that a prophetic day = a literal year, 483 *prophetic* days = 483 *literal* years.

When understood in the context of the day-for-a-year principle, Daniel's time prophecy predicted the Messiah some 483 years from his time. The English word "Messiah" in Daniel 9:25, 26 is literally "anointed one" in Hebrew (*Strong's* #4899). Applying this day-for-a-year principle would mean that the Messiah would appear and be baptized in the early 1st century AD, just as Christ was. Yet biblical prophecy is always supported by historical fact, which is why we have the Daniel-Luke connection.

The Two Caesars

1st century AD historical data in the book of Luke nails this prophecy! First, Luke records the birth of Christ under Augustus Caesar. Then Luke records the baptism of Christ under Tiberius Caesar. Two very significant Roman rulers are identified by name to establish Daniel's prophetic date.

These biblical and historical records affirming the day-for-year application to Daniel's prophetic timeline are found in Luke's account of the birth and baptism of Jesus:

"And it came to pass in those days, that there went out a decree from Caesar Augustus, that all the world should be taxed. (And this taxing was first made when Cyrenius was governor of Syria.) And all went to be taxed, every one into his own city. And Joseph also went up from Galilee, out of the city of Nazareth, into Judaea, unto the city of David, which is called Bethlehem; (because he was of the house and lineage of David) to be taxed with Mary his espoused wife, being great with child" (Luke 2:1-5).

This account connects Christ's birth to the reign of

Augustus Caesar (BC 27 to AD 14). The next Scripture reference gives us the historical year for the baptism of Jesus:

"Now in the fifteenth year of the reign of Tiberius Caesar, Pontius Pilate being governor of Judea, Herod being tetrarch of Galilee, his brother Philip tetrarch of Iturea and the region of Trachonitis, and Lysanias tetrarch of Abilene, while Annas and Caiaphas were high priests, the word of God came to John the son of Zacharias in the wilderness. And he went into all the region around the Jordan, preaching a baptism of repentance for the remission of sins, as it is written in the book of the words of Isaiah the prophet, saying: 'The voice of one crying in the wilderness: 'Prepare the way of the LORD; make His paths straight'" (Luke 3:1-4, NKJV).

Luke's detailed historical account not only of Augustus and Tiberius, but also of the local governor, rulers, and high priests, is intentional and unique to his gospel. His purpose to establish a timeframe for Christ's birth and then to His baptism is evident.

"When all the people were baptized, it came to pass that Jesus also was baptized; and while He prayed, the heaven was opened. And the Holy Spirit descended in bodily form like a dove upon Him, and a voice came from heaven which said, 'You are My beloved Son; in You I am well pleased.' Now Jesus

Himself began *His ministry at* about thirty years of age" (Luke 3:21-23, NKJV).

In giving us this timeframe in connection with these events, Luke confirms Daniel's Messianic time prophecy by pinpointing the very year that Christ was anointed by the Holy Spirit. The 15ᵗʰ year of the reign of Tiberius Caesar is the biblical marker for the baptism of Jesus. In yet another intentional ink-to-papyrus moment of inspirational genius, Luke connects the account of Christ's baptism to the anointing of the Holy Spirit:

"The word which God sent to the children of Israel, preaching peace through Jesus Christ—He is Lord of all—that word you know, which was proclaimed throughout all Judea, and began from Galilee after the baptism which John preached: how *God anointed Jesus of Nazareth with the Holy Spirit and with power*, who went about doing good and healing all who were oppressed by the devil, for God was with Him" (Acts 10:36-38, NKJV).

We learned earlier that the word "Messiah" in Daniel means the "anointed one." So Luke's intention was to establish the historicity of the Messiah, the very year of Christ's baptism and anointing by the Holy Spirit, beyond any doubt. (It was just after His baptism that John also recorded Jesus as "the Messias, which is being interpreted, the Christ" John 1:41.)

The book of Daniel *predicted the event* over 400 years before it happened.

The book of Luke *confirmed the event* over 400 years later, as it happened.

According to the Old and New Testament records, Jesus was anointed with the Holy Spirit exactly 483 years after the beginning of the 70-week prophecy in Daniel 9. This anointing is the end-point of the 483 years to "Messiah the Prince."

Chart 2

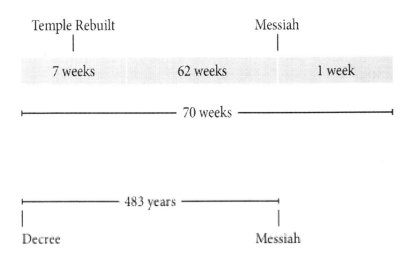

The 15th Year of Tiberius Caesar

Historical accounts of the 15th year of the reign of Tiberius Caesar take us to the year AD 27. The following statements are easy-to-find references that pinpoint the beginning of the reign of Tiberius to AD 13:

1. "From A.D. 4 to 14 Tiberius was clearly Augustus's successor. When he was adopted, he also received grants of proconsular power and tribunician power; and in A.D. 13 his proconsular power was made co-extensive with that of Augustus. In effect, Tiberius was now co-princeps with Augustus so that when the latter finally died on 19 August A.D. 14, Tiberius's position was unassailable and the continuation of the Principate a foregone conclusion. After 55 years living at the behest of his stepfather, Tiberius finally assumed the mantle of sole power" (Suet. *Tib*. 21.1; Vell. 2.121.1.: http://www.luc.edu/roman-emperors/tiberius.htm).

2. "In his later years, Augustus withdrew more and more from the public eye, although he continued to transact public business. He was getting older, and old age in ancient times must have been considerably more debilitating than it is today. In any case, Tiberius had been installed as his successor and, by AD 13, was virtually emperor already. In AD 4 he had received grants of both proconsular and tribunician power, which had been renewed as a matter of course whenever they needed to be; in AD 13, Tiberius's *imperium* had been made co-extensive with that of Augustus" (http://www.luc.edu/roman-emperors/auggie.htm).

3. "In that year, Tiberius was also granted the powers of a tribune and proconsul, emissaries from foreign kings had to pay their respects to him, and by [AD] 13 was awarded with his second triumph and equal level of *imperium* with that of Augustus" (Augustus Caesar, from Wikipedia, the free encyclopedia: http://en.wikipedia.org/wiki/Augustus).

4. "In AD 13 Tiberius' constitutional powers were renewed on equal terms with those of Augustus, making his succession inevitable, as the elderly Augustus died in AD 14" (http://www.roman-empire.net/emperors/tiberius.html).

5. "The last year of his life, Augustus shared

the rule with Tiberius and when he died, Tiberius was voted emperor by the senate" (http://ancienthistory.about.com/od/emperors /ig/12-Caesars/Tiberius-.htm).

Tiberius began his reign as "co-princeps" with Augustus Caesar in AD 13, the year before the death of Augustus in AD 14. This, then, was the first year of the rule of Tiberius Caesar.

Counting 15 years forward from AD 13 takes us to AD 27 as noted in the following outline:

AD 13=1st yr   AD 14=2nd yr

AD 15=3rd yr   AD 16=4th yr

AD 17=5th yr   AD 18=6th yr

AD 19=7th yr   AD 20=8th yr

AD 21=9th yr   AD 22=10th yr

AD 23=11th yr   AD 24=12th yr

AD 25=13th yr   AD 26=14th yr

AD 27=15th yr

According to Luke's inspired account of biblical history, Jesus was anointed *in* the 15th year of the reign of Tiberius Caesar, establishing the prophetic reckoning made by Daniel:

"From the going forth of the command to restore and build Jerusalem until Messiah the Prince, there shall be seven weeks and sixty-two weeks" (Daniel 9:25, NKJV).

The 69 prophetic weeks translates into 483 literal years (applying the day-for-a-year principle of prophetic interpretation—69 weeks = 483 *prophetic* days/*literal* years).

So from AD 27, the 15th year of the reign of Tiberius Caesar, we simply count back 483 literal years to find the beginning date for the 70-week prophecy:

483 years
– AD 27
= BC 456
– 1 (for zero year)
= BC 457

CHART 3

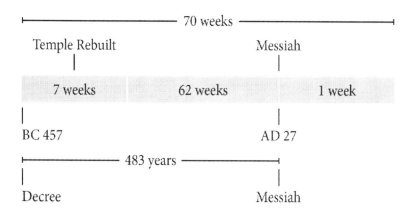

This is not complicated math. If we start counting back 483 years from AD 27, we arrive at BC 457.

AD 27 = 483	AD 26 = 482
AD 25 = 481	AD 24 = 480
AD 23 = 479	AD 22 = 478
AD 21 = 477	AD 20 = 476
AD 19 = 475	AD 18 = 474
AD 17 = 473	AD 16 = 472
AD 15 = 471	AD 14 = 470
AD 13 = 469	AD 12 = 468

AD 11 = 467   AD 10 = 466

AD 9 = 465   AD 8 = 464

AD 7 = 463   AD 6 = 462

AD 5 = 461   AD 4 = 460

AD 3 = 459   AD 2 = 458

AD 1 = 457

AD 0 = no zero year in history

BC 1 = 456

BC 1 + 456 = BC 457

CHART 4

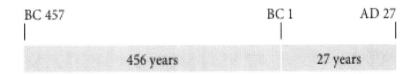

We double check the above equation with a different approach. Instead of subtracting 27 from 483, we can add 27 and 457 as follows:

27 + 457 = 484.

Then we subtract one year, in the transition from AD to BC. Since there is no zero year between AD and BC, AD 1 becomes BC 1 in one year. So 484 subtract 1 = 483. Both of these equations lead to the same simple conclusion:

In AD 27 Jesus was anointed with the Holy Spirit, precisely 483 years from BC 457.

Either way we do the math we arrive at the same simple conclusion. Based on Luke's gospel account of Jesus' birth and baptism, we have the fulfillment of the prophecy of Daniel pinpointing the anointing of Jesus as the Messiah 483 years after the decree to build Jerusalem. Historical data confirms that the 15th year of Tiberius Caesar was the year AD 27. According to New Testament record, Jesus was anointed in AD 27. Tracing back 483 years from the year AD 27 brings us to BC 457. This, then, would be the starting point of the 2300-day prophecy, which solidly nails down the ending point as 1844!

The Messiah

So far the interpretation of the 70 weeks leaves seven literal years (the 70th prophetic week) for the complete fulfillment of the 70-week prophecy. According to the context of Daniel's prophecy this 70th week was to include the death of the Messiah:

"And after [seven weeks, verse 25 and*] the sixty-two weeks Messiah shall be cut off, but not for Himself" (Daniel 9:25, 26, NKJV).

"In the midst of the week, He shall cause the sacrifice and the oblation to cease" (Daniel 9:27).

It was to be *after* the 69 weeks (483 literal years), in the "middle" of the remaining week (3 ½ years into the 70th week), that Christ was to be "cut off" (Daniel 9:26, 27). Precisely 3 ½ years after His baptism, in the middle of the 70th week, Christ would give His life as the ultimate sacrifice for the sin of the world. This sacrifice is the capstone of the 70-week prophetic time line. The prophecy allotted 70 weeks to "finish the transgression . . . make an end of sins . . . make reconciliation for iniquity, and . . . bring in everlasting righteousness." Christ, and

ONLY Christ, could accomplish these tasks. This is why Daniel was told to:

"KNOW THEREFORE AND UNDERSTAND, that from the going forth of the command to restore and build Jerusalem until Messiah the Prince, there shall be seven weeks and sixty-two weeks" (Daniel 9:25, NKJV).

Daniel was to "know and understand" that Messiah was to come in 483 years because only Messiah could finish transgressions, make an end of sin, and make reconciliation for iniquity BEFORE the allotted 490 years (70 weeks) were to end! The Messiah would be anointed after 483 years and then He would be "cut off, but not for Himself," 3 ½ years later, in the middle of the final week. The Messiah is the only way transgression, sin, and iniquity could be finished and the only way everlasting righteousness could be brought in.

This, then, is a second biblical affirmation that Jesus is Messiah. The two foundational biblical facts are as follows:

1. The historical data outlined by the prophecies of Daniel and confirmed by the historical accounts in Luke, as well as a number of extra biblical historical sources, lead directly to Christ.

2. Christ ALONE accomplished every

specification of the prophecy as it applies to salvation. Only Jesus Christ has atoned for the transgression, sin, and iniquity of the world, bringing us the gift of His everlasting righteousness.

Jesus is the only one who meets every specification of Daniel's prophecy, therefore He is the only One who can be the Messiah! This is a key point of prophetic interpretation. First, Jesus came at the right time, historically and prophetically. Second, He did what no human being ever has or ever will do. He single-handedly saved the world. Glory to God!

The 70-week prophecy cannot be applied to any other place or person because Jesus alone meets all it specifications and fulfills all its predictions.

The application of this prophecy to Jesus becomes vitally clear when we understand the message of the everlasting gospel that brings salvation from sin through Jesus Christ. Scrap the gospel, and the interpretation of this prophecy is unsure. Understand the gospel, and you "seal up the vision and prophecy" (Daniel 9:24).

Seal the Vision—This last phrase, "seal up the vision and prophecy," suggests two separate aspects of this prophecy that are closely connected. The first is the "vision" that Daniel saw. This prophetic "vision" applies to Jesus. It is sealed up in

Him. No person other than Jesus Christ can fulfill it.

Seal the Prophecy—The sealing up of the "prophecy" refers to the time element. Not only does the vision apply to Jesus, but the time element of prophecy points to AD 27. From this date we also confirm BC 457 and AD 31, as well as AD 34 and finally AD 1844. The 2300-day/70-week time prophecy is sealed in the life, the anointing, and the death of Jesus.

The vision is sealed up in that it applies to Jesus. The prophecy is sealed up in that it applies from BC 457 to AD 1844, both of these dates centered in the pivotal AD 27 date. Both the vision and the prophecy are sealed and centered in the Messiah!

The gospel of Christ makes the 70-week prophecy not only a message about time, but *the* message of *all* time.

CHART 5

2300 Prophetic Day/Literal Year Prophecy

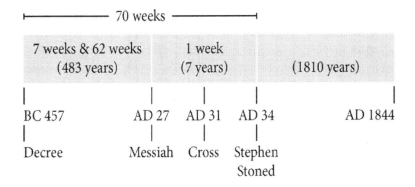

Additional New Testament Evidence

Luke was more intentional in recording the historical data that affirms Daniel's Messianic time prophecy, but other New Testament writers were also inspired to record key information affirming the fulfillment of this prophetic time. Mark's gospel account records these words of Jesus just after His baptism:

"The *time* is fulfilled, and the kingdom of God is at hand: repent ye, and believe the gospel" (Mark 1:15).

The only "time" Jesus could be referring to is the 483-year portion of the 70-week prophecy set by Gabriel to point out the very year of His anointing as the Messiah at His baptism. This is extremely significant because it means that Jesus knew Daniel's prophecy and knew He was its fulfillment. It is also significant because this means that Jesus explicitly confirms the day-for-a-year principle of prophetic interpretation, which by extension means that Jesus confirmed that Daniel's time prophecy would, indeed, reach to its end point in 1844.

Both Matthew and John also had something to say about the Messianic time prophecy. They record the actions of Jesus between His baptism and His death. This timeframe constitutes the 70th week of the 70-week time prophecy. It was during this 70th week that Christ was to be "cut off, but not for Himself." Both New Testament writers note that Jesus referred, on several occasions, to a cryptic "time" that helped guide the last actions of His life. For example, when the hour had come for Him to be "cut off" for our sins, Matthew records Christ saying to His disciples:

"Go into the city to such a man, and say unto him, 'The Master saith, My *time* is at hand; I will keep the Passover at thy house with My disciples'" (Matthew 26:18).

In this statement Jesus affirms the 70-week prophecy as though it were a message from Father to Son, directing Him to Calvary. Earlier in His ministry when urged to openly declare Himself as the Messiah, the very thing that led to His death,

John records Jesus' declaration:

"My *time* is not yet come" (John 7:6).

And again:

"My *time* is not yet full come" (John 7:8).

The New Testament record is in perfect harmony with the Old Testament prophecy. Christ knew when His time had come and when it had not. He understood His prophetic destiny. He knew that His death could not, would not, take place until the time had arrived to fulfill the 70-week prophecy, which is why earlier attempts to take Christ's life always failed.

The apostle Paul was inspired to add his endorsement to the placement of this time prophecy when he said:

"For when we were yet without strength, in *due time* Christ died for the ungodly" (Romans 5:6).

And again:

"Who gave Himself a ransom for all, to be testified in *due time*" (1 Timothy 2:6, NKJV).

It is significant that the word *time* in these texts is coupled with the word "*due,*" thus adding additional weight to the application of the 70-week prophecy that was established through the angel Gabriel in Daniel 8 and 9.

God gave Gabriel this awesome message to communicate to His humble servant Daniel. After explaining the prophecy to Daniel, over 400 years pass until finally the time for the Messiah arrives. Gabriel is enlisted again and given the privilege of communicating the fulfillment of this same prophetic promise to Planet Earth. We can only imagine how excited Gabriel must have felt. No wonder he put Zacharias on a time-out for his unbelief. Gabriel had been waiting for this day for over 400 years and all Zacharias could do was voice his doubts. Few recognized the Gabriel connection. Few understood that Christ had be born, anointed, and crucified in exact fulfillment of the 70-week prophecy. Daniel, Luke, Mark, Matthew, John, Paul and Jesus stand together in support of the greatest news ever proclaimed to Planet Earth, the consummation of the 70-week prophecy that pointed to the sacrifice of Christ for our sins:

"In the midst of the week He shall cause the sacrifice and the oblation to cease" (Daniel 9:27).

The seventieth week takes us seven literal years beyond AD 27 to AD 34. In the middle of this 70th week Christ was crucified (AD 31). Matthew says that at Christ's death "the veil of the temple was torn in two from top to bottom" (Matthew 27:51, NKJV). This supernatural act of God announced the end of the sacrifices in the earthly sanctuary service. The sacrifices typified Christ, the ultimate sacrifice for sin. They pointed to Messiah as the Lamb of God who takes away the sin of the world (John 1:29; 1 Corinthians 5:7).

The 70th week ends in AD 34. In this year Stephen is stoned, signaling the rejection of the gospel by the Jews as a nation. This is why Stephen's last words recounting the history of Israel were in the form of a judicial indictment for their sins, a closing judgment of sorts to the 70-week prophecy (Acts 7). Before His departure Christ had told His disciples to go first to the house of Israel (Matthew 10:6; 13:46). After the stoning of Stephen the early church was "scattered abroad" and "went every where preaching the word" (Acts 8:4).

A rebuke from Christ directed at the Pharisees offers another piece of evidence directing us to the fulfillment of the 70-week prophecy. These religious leaders boasted to have great prophetic knowledge, and yet they would not "discern this time" (Luke 12:56). The rebuke is even more significant because Luke is the only gospel writer to record it. One cannot help but connect this rebuke to Luke's careful historical record that clearly establishes the timeframe of the 70-week prophecy. The Jews should have been aware of this prophecy, but they failed to make the application of the timeline to Jesus. They refused to acknowledge Jesus as "Messiah the Prince."

Luke further records the prophetic words of Jesus to future generations warning that this same neglect to discern the prophetic Messianic timeline would be repeated. False religious teachers would say, "the time draweth near" (Luke 21:8). Christ's warning points to false religious teachers even today. They, like the religious leaders before them, misapply the 70-week prophecy, teaching that it is yet to be fulfilled in the future when its actual fulfillment has already happened in Christ. Confirmation of Christ's warning can be found in the "Left Behind" enthusiasm that has taken much of the evangelical world by storm. The Jews misapplied the prophecies of the Messiah to their hope for a conquering Christ. Today, the 70th week of Daniel's prophecy is being misapplied to a conquering Antichrist. Both interpretations fail to connect Daniel's time prophecies to Jesus Christ.

The sure word of prophecy centers Daniel's 70-weeks prophecy in Jesus—His love and His forgiveness. The Messiah has come right on time as God said He would and has taken care of our sins, transgressions, and iniquities, just as prophetically promised.

Thank you Jesus!

Summary

The gospel of Luke records the reign of Augustus and Tiberius Caesar, giving us the exact year of the baptism of Jesus and His anointing as the Messiah in AD 27. Tracing the prophecy of Daniel back from this date 483 prophetic days/literal years takes us to BC 457. This, then, is the beginning date of the 70-week/2300-day prophecy, thus pointing to Messiah the Prince, who would come to:

1. "to finish the transgression,

2. and to make an end of sins,

3. and to make reconciliation for iniquity,

4. and to bring an everlasting righteousness,

5. and to seal up the vision

6. and prophecy,

7. and to anoint the most Holy" (Daniel 9:24).

Only Christ could have fulfilled this prophecy to the letter. The Messiah accomplished the tasks that no other even could. The application to Jesus Christ is profound, accurate, and sure. It announces the greatest act of self-sacrificing love ever manifested in the universe. Time prophecy is not boring mathematics. In Christ it becomes the only hope for humanity.

Amen.

Evidence for AD 34

The 70th week takes us to AD 34. It was in this year that Stephen was stoned to death. This signaled the rejection of the gospel by the Jews as a nation. Before His departure Christ had told His disciples to go first to the house of Israel (Matthew 10:6; 13:46). After the stoning of Stephen the early church was "scattered abroad" and "went every where preaching the word" (Acts 8:4).

According to the following biblical and historical evidence, Stephen was stoned in AD 34, at the end of the 70th week of the prophecy in Daniel 9. When Stephen was stoned, Saul (later Paul) was not only consenting to his death, but also led out in the following persecution that scattered the church abroad (Acts 7:58; 8:1, 22:20). As Saul went to Damascus to persecute the church he was converted by a direct encounter with Jesus (Acts

9:1-16). Three years after his conversion in AD 34, Saul, now Paul, visited Jerusalem to see Peter (Galatians 1:18). Then some 14 years later Paul returned to Jerusalem with Barnabas and Titus (Galatians 2:1). This would add 17 years to AD 34, bringing us to AD 51. A short time before his final visit to Jerusalem, Paul stood before Gallio, as recorded in Acts 18:12-17. Gallio was the deputy of Achaia when Paul was brought to the judgment seat.

Historical records indicate the following:

"Gallio (originally named Lucius Annaeus Novatus) was the son of the rhetorician Seneca the Elder and the elder brother of Seneca the Younger, was born at Corduba (Cordova) about the beginning of the Christian era . . . According to the book of Acts he dismissed the charge brought by the Jews against the Apostle Paul (Acts 18:12-17). His behaviour on this occasion ('but Gallio cared for none of these things,' v. 17) showed his disregard for Jewish sensitivities, and also the impartial attitude of Roman officials towards Christianity in its early days. Gallio's tenure can be fairly accurately dated to between AD 51-52. Therefore, the events of Acts 18 can be dated to this period. This is significant because it is the most accurately known date in the life of Paul" (http://en.wikipedia.org/wiki/Lucius_Junius_Gallio _Annaeanus).

"View of the portion of the 'Gallio Inscription' from Delphi that mentions Gallio. In the large fragment, in the fourth line from the top, the Greek form of 'Gallio' is clearly visible. Gallio was the proconsul of Achaia while Paul was in Corinth (Acts 18:12). The inscription is written in Greek and is a copy of a decree of the Roman Emperor Claudius (AD 41–54) who commanded L. Iunius Gallio, the governor, to assist in settling additional elite persons in Delphi—in an effort to revitalize it. The inscription dates between April and July AD, 52, and from it, it can be deduced that Gallio was the proconsul of Achaia in the previous year. Thus Paul's eighteenth month stay in Corinth (Acts 18:1–18) included the year 51. This inscription is critical in helping to establish the chronology of Paul as presented in the book of Acts" (http://holylandphotos.org/browse.asp?s=1,4,11,28,74,95&img=GCTCDLAR15; see also *Evidence for God*, p. 227, William Dembski, Michael Licona, Baker Books, 2010).

Paul stood before Gallio in 51 AD, exactly 17 years after His conversion (immediately after Stephen was stoned Paul was converted). Take 51 AD and subtract 17 and it leaves 34 AD, which is the year Stephen was stoned. Stephen's reckoning of the history of Israel and his subsequent martyrdom closed the 70-week prophetic period, which had been "determined" or "cut off" for Israel. Read it, research it, believe it, share it!

Made in United States
Troutdale, OR
11/26/2024

25283190R00027